W9-CXQ-451

# Alive and Awake

## WISDOM *for* Kids

Other books by Dianne M. Connelly:

*All Sickness Is Home Sickness*

*Traditional Acupuncture: The Law of the Five Elements*

# Alive and Awake
## WISDOM *for* Kids

Dianne M. Connelly
and Katherine Hancock Porter

**Illustrations by Melora Scanlon**

**Tai Sophia Institute**
for the **Healing Arts**
7750 Montpelier Road
Laurel, Maryland 20723

ALIVE AND AWAKE: WISDOM FOR KIDS
Copyright © 2003 by Dianne M. Connelly and
Katherine Hancock Porter

Published by Tai Sophia Press

All rights reserved. No part of this work may be reproduced or transmitted in any form or by any means, electronic or mechanical, including photocopying and recording, or by any information storage and retrieval system, except as may be expressly permitted by the 1976 Copyright Act or in writing from the publisher. To request permission, write to:

        Tai Sophia Institute
        7750 Montpelier Road
        Laurel, Maryland 20723-6010

Printed in the United States of America

Illustrations: Melora Scanlon
Book design: John C. Wilson
Photograph of authors: Carol Cathcart
Production editing and coordination: Nancy C. Thompson
Editor: Mary Ellen Zorbaugh
Copy editors: Elizabeth Scanlon and Guy Hollyday

Library of Congress Control Number: 2003116028

ISBN 0-912381-05-1

# Table of Contents

# For the Sake of the Kids

One spring morning, Dianne stood in a circle of children assembled for a workshop on Chinese philosophy:

> I walked in front of each child, looking into his or her eyes, and then rang a bell to each one in turn. I do this at the beginning of every workshop and class I teach—usually it is with adults sitting in a circle. As I stood in front of eight-year-old, red-headed Charlie, I rang the bell and he blurted out,
>
> "Whadya do that for?"
>
> In all these years of teaching workshops, no adult had ever asked me that. I paused a moment, then asked,
>
> "Well Charlie, what did you notice?"
>
> "I woke up!" he said.

By ringing the bell in front of each person, I intend it as a wake-up call, a "yoo-hoo" to being here this moment. Awake to being alive here and now with others. Awake to being mortal, to dwelling here on the earth until our call comes and we have to go. The bell is a reminder to give our attention, our sacred awareness, to each other. And so Charlie spontaneously saying "I woke up!" is a gift to all of us. By his observation, "I woke up!," we each receive a wake-up call. As Charlie recognizes *that* he is awake, he can observe some new possibilities about being alive. And so can we all.

This is a book of stories like the one above—by and about children who are in the practice of being alive and awake. They are presented here as teaching stories or parables. Many of these stories come from days spent with children in a "workshop" setting. Others come from years of treating children with acupuncture—things they have said in conversations in the treatment room. We intend that you, dear reader, use these stories as seeds for conversations, for gatherings with children who are in life with you.

These parables are also intended to illustrate some of the "bones," i.e., philosophical underpinnings, of Chinese philosophy for anyone who comes in contact with this book, no matter what his or her age. For whether we are one or 100, eight or 80, three or 30, as long as we have breath we are in the glorious adventure of being. We are all, as Joni Mitchell says, "aging children." We beings of the human sort in this adventure of living are full of thoughts and concerns about what it is to be. We turn our thoughts into practices—practices to bring more ease to being alive, practices for being more wakeful to being alive.

From where did we glean these practices and these "bones"? A human philosophy came into being through the ancient Chinese by observing nature. The ancient Chinese were agrarian people—farmers of the land who were reverent toward the earth. As such, they were keen observers of nature and the seasons. In our current era, the seasons still show us practices, some gifts to live by as we become more observant.

Many years ago, my colleague-friends Jack, Julia, Haig, Bob, Erica and I (Dianne) founded a school to train people how to do acupuncture. Over time, some of the folks we treated came to us saying that they wanted access to our acupuncture training program. They said: "We don't want to be acupuncturists, but we do want to learn what you know, what you have to offer. We don't want to learn to use the needle, we want to learn to *be* the needle. You are being irresponsible with what you have if you do not make this philosophy available outside the treatment room, for all the rooms of life—bedrooms, boardrooms, classrooms, living rooms, everywhere there are beings of the human sort. This thinking belongs to all of us."

From this call we created SOPHIA, the School of Philosophy and Healing in Action. "Philosophy" because we used the ideas, the "bones," of Chinese philosophy. The ancient Greek roots of this word—*philia* meaning love, and *sophos* meaning wisdom—make up the word philosophy, the "love of wisdom." SOPHIA is based on a human wisdom brought forth for all of us by Chinese farmers long ago who observed and learned life as nature. "Healing" because our life is always about being in service of others, honoring their wholeness. Healing is actually acknowledging the wholeness in one another. And, "Action," because it is through our actions, our words, the movements we make and the gifts we give that we come alive and recognize that we are dwelling here on earth, embodied. And we are here together. Our intention in SOPHIA is, as John Sullivan has written, "To come to life more fully, so as to serve life more wisely and more nobly. Sagely stillness within, sovereign service without."

How could we be more wise and noble with our children? We imprison our kids with labels, assessments negative or positive—sentencing our youngsters to being all and always one way or another: "underdeveloped," "overachiever," "attention deficit disorder," "straight-A genius," "learning disabled," "rowdy," "shy," "good," "bad," until our kids think of themselves as those labels, and often as problems. We and they miss their very *being*, and yet each child has never been before and will never be again; they are unique. Each of us has our "squawks," and we are not our squawks. We are so much more than labels or squawks. What would it take for us to see every child as a gift no matter what? And every squawk or problem as an offering in disguise? This book stands for the possibility of heeding any label applied to any kid as a wake-up call to all of us to learn new ways of being alive and awake together.

Many folks who have taken part in SOPHIA over the years asked if it was available for children, for the "youngers" among us. And so came a birthing of SOPHIA for Kids.* Having put together day-long SOPHIA workshops for kids, we realized that the children are great teachers for all of us, no matter what our

*When the pickpocket sees the Saint on the road, all the pickpocket sees are the Saint's pockets!*

—Old Chinese saying

age. We can learn from their example, from their stories; and anyone of any age can take this philosophy and put it to use. *Through this book you will create ways to bring what is presented here into actions, actions you can put into practice immediately.*

We, Dianne and Katherine, write this book in the form of teaching stories, an easy and useful way to share this philosophy with you, our partners, our readers. Practice with those in life with you. Use the suggested activities as a springboard for other ways to anchor these teachings through practices.

We observe that the offerings we are making are gifts *from* the kids to you, the readers, as well as *for* the kids. This book is for all-age kids, age one to 120. Our intention is to bring into words the "goods," the offerings of the children, and then deliver them as parables for living.

> *Don't go back to sleep.*
> —Rumi

> *It would be a mistake not to wake up before we die.*
> —Hindu saying

---

* Since SOPHIA is the Greek word for wisdom, we titled this book "Alive and Awake, Wisdom for Kids."

# How to Use this Book:

## An Overview of Chinese Philosophy

Before sharing the distinctions of ancient Chinese philosophy with kids, you will need to have some understanding yourself of the principles you will share with them. The teaching stories contained in this book are illustrations of one or more of these basic "bones." These are the underpinnings of a philosophy that is more than 5,000 years old—ancient and yet infinitely adaptable and useful in our modern time.

You may be surprised at how simple and commonsensical it is. In fact, the basis of it is as simple as counting, literally, One, Two, Three, Four, Five. Notice that we are counting by One. "One" shows itself as Two – Three – Four – Five. Two remembering (plus) One (the Oneness) is Three. Three remembering One is Four. Four remembering One is Five.

# ONE *Remembering We Are One*

The first principle, or "bone" as we are calling them here, of Chinese philosophy, the principle that underscores all others, is Oneness. You may have heard it referred to elsewhere as the "Tao." It can be a challenging principle to explain in words or images. In fact, the ancient Chinese wisdom text, the Tao Te Ching, written approximately 2,500 years ago, begins: "The Tao that can be spoken is not the Tao." Oneness may be thought of as a prior unity, a unity that exists by declaration no matter what the appearance. Whitecaps on the surface of the ocean may appear as separate waves, yet just a bit beneath the surface they are all made up of the same ocean. It is the same for human beings and all of life: we are each aspects of the same ultimate whole. One is the knowledge of a union or unity with all of life and all things. As we look upon one another we can realize that we actually share atoms. My breath taken in by you becomes part of you, you become part of me. This goes on day in and day out throughout the world. A week or two goes by and we have incorporated atoms from others in China or Africa. This is just one of the ways in which we are all One.

Oneness is not so much to be analyzed or understood as experienced and recognized. Many of us have had an experience when we perceived that we are not separate from what surrounds us. You may have known this in a moment of intimacy with another person. You might sense this at times during particularly powerful artistic performances—for instance, when the audience comes together in a shared moment and acts as one being, rising all at once in a standing ovation. We may find ourselves looking into the smiling eyes of someone and simply smiling back....

You may have perceived Oneness while being out-of-doors in nature. The poet William Wordsworth described such an experience in his poem "Lines Composed A Few Miles Above Tintern Abbey":

> ...*And I have felt*
> *A presence that disturbs me with the joy*
> *Of elevated thoughts; a sense sublime*
> *Of something far more deeply interfused,*
> *Whose dwelling is the light of setting suns,*
> *And the round ocean, and the living air,*
> *And the blue sky...*
> *A motion and a spirit, that impels*
> *All thinking things, all objects of all thought,*
> *And rolls through all things....*

You may have noticed this sense of peacefulness and connection while watching the ocean or looking into the eyes of a newborn baby. Often folks experience this connection with animal companions. Imagine a horse and rider moving in graceful harmony. This is all we mean by One in this text. As we write about experiencing Oneness we often use words such as "instant" or "moment." Also, in the examples we have used, we write as if it is something that just "happens" for a rare and fleeting interval and then departs as mysteriously as it came. For many of us it seems this way. One of the most important bones of philosophy in this book is that cultivating our awareness of Oneness is a practice. The more we remind ourselves of this prior unity with all beings and all things, the more peacefulness and ease we will generate.

We practice Oneness not as a pleasant idea or concept to employ when it is convenient and only with those we "like." Notice that the very times when opposition or struggle occur are the moments crying out for us to remember that we are One with another. Our practice for the sake of the children must be that this Oneness is literally always so. What might shift if you reminded yourself of Oneness at the very second when you perceived the most separation? Begin with something small: the next time someone cuts you off in traffic and you begin your usual reaction, think instead, "I am One with that driver." See what you notice. Oneness is always and eternally present. It is we who forget. What we experience as separation or opposition is a longing to be reminded of this prior unity. It is so by declaration: "I am One with . . ." because I declare it so.

## A Practice of Oneness

Point your finger toward your own body and say "I am pointing to myself." Keep saying "I am pointing to myself" and point your finger toward another. Really look at that human being when you say this. Really mean it.

Now, keep saying "I am pointing to myself," and point to a tree, the sky, the earth beneath your feet, an animal.

# TWO *The Dance of Partnership*

You may have heard of the idea of yin-yang and seen this symbol.

The ancient picture for yin-yang was a mountain with one side in sun and the other side in shadow: the play of light and dark; a cooler side and a warmer side. Both the light and the dark are facets of the same thing—they are both sides of the same Oneness of the mountain. Two is always about One. Sometimes you may hear yin and yang described as opposites. Opposition is a misunderstanding of yin-yang. Rather, they are mutually arising and complementary. We cannot know what dark is without some experience of light. We do not know cold without hot. There is no yang without yin. We all experience this. Sometimes we are quiet and more like the shady side of the mountain. At times we are active and bright, more like the sunny side. In a given day we begin as still and sleeping, we awaken into activity, and at the end of the day return to stillness. We go up and down just as there is dark and light and then dark again. In being with another, one may speak while the other listens. There is no speaking without listening, just as there is no sound without silence. In the movement of yin-yang, the Two is the dance of partnership. Sometimes this dance looks like opposition rather than partnership. Sometimes we both want to speak at once without listening to the other. When that happens it is a call to the partnership of the Two. We declare our Oneness and become Two remembering One.

## A Practice of "Two"

Choose a partner and music for dancing. Play the music. One dancer leads and the other follows. Now trade roles. Observe how the two of you dance: leading and following; stillness and movement; being and doing. All of these are examples of the dance of Two.

# Three *The Movement of Ch'i*

The ancient Chinese had a word for life that is not readily translated into English. That word is Ch'i. The English words that come closest to it are breath, life force, animation, vapor, vitality, movement—that without which we are dead. The Chinese character for Ch'i (気) is derived from the image of a pot full of rice cooking over a fire.

    All the ways that life moves are present in this image. As the flames cook the rice, steam rises from beneath the lid. This steam bubbles and the lid of the rice pot moves up and down. From the up and down movement of the rice pot lid (comparable to the dance of yin-yang) a third thing arises: the action, the breath, the vapor of the steam that is the movement of life itself. Our goal is not to have the rice pot lid stay closed; the rice would get too hot and burn. We do not take the lid off the pot, for the rice might not cook enough. Our intention is to keep the lid moving up and down so that the rice cooks. Three is this movement—life on the move. We may experience this movement as the creation of a new third thing when in partnership with another. For instance, we (Two) came together to write this book. Each of us took turns writing, and reading what the other had written. In the end this third thing, the book you hold in your hands, was created for the sake of the whole (One).

    Sometimes the movement of Three can get stuck, and we can see no movement or vitality in what we are creating. We can get it moving again by going back to the partnership of the Two.

## A Practice of "Three"

Get a scarf and choose a partner. Each of you takes one end of the scarf, holding it with just enough tension to allow you to feel the other person move. Now, one person pulls the scarf tight so there is no give to it. Does it feel "stuck"? Then both of you work together to allow some movement. Next, allow slack so that you cannot feel the other person move. Once again increase the tension so you feel the movement. This play shows ways of ease and movement.

# Four
## *The Directions: North, South, East, West*

Four is the number of the directions: North, South, East, West. It is in the directions that the movement of Three continues— life is on the move with the Ch'i naturally flowing to and from all the places of the earth. Movement requires place or space into which to move. Without the directions, movement could not occur.

In many Native traditions, any action begins in a prayer honoring the gods and goddesses of the Four directions. This practice recognizes the unity of the earth by acknowledging that each of the directions is equally important.

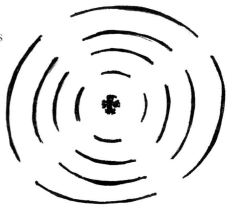

The movement of the Three naturally gives birth to Four. Farmers must take their fruit to the marketplace in order to nourish those who need their produce, and be nourished in turn by the exchange. In the same way, people take their thoughts, ideas, and spoken words to the marketplace of living. We influence one another by sending our ideas out into the world and having them return to us.

### A Practice of "Four"
With a partner, create something that interests you. It can be food, a picture, a poem, anything creative. Both of you sit with the finished product, just the two of you. Then share it with two to four other people. Notice the difference in the experience when it is just the two creators and when it is shared with "the world."

# Five
## Our Five Senses

From the simplicity of the One, the partnership of the Two, the movement of the Three, and the direction of the Four, we now move to Five. The ancient Chinese observed Five seasons of the year: Winter, Spring, Summer, Late Summer, and Autumn. They noticed that each of these seasons had a particular quality and movement of its own. Each is distinct and yet always in relationship to the others, always a part of the whole cycle, the Oneness. As we see the cycle of seasons in a year, so can we observe the cycle in all aspects of life. All of these gifts are expressions of what it means to be. Each of the seasons is a facet of the seamless fabric of existence. We distinguish the seasons from one another in order to see the whole of the circle of life, and to learn to live in awe, in "perpetual great astonishment."

In this philosophy, beings of the human sort are as much a part of nature as a tree, a river, or an animal. And thus the same movements of nature apply to us. Each season is associated with one of the five senses: hearing, seeing, touching, tasting, and smelling. And each season has a particular gift or offering. The simplest way to understand this idea is to look at what you already know of each season through your own experience.

Since the cycle of seasons has no beginning or ending, we could start anywhere. The cycle is present in everyone and everything, so let us ponder the idea of growing tomatoes. Let's begin with the season of Winter.

The Winter is cold with longer nights and shorter days. There is a quality of stillness all around us in nature. Plants are hidden under the snows; trees are bare; animals hibernate or migrate. During the winter, seeds rest under the cold dark ground. We can't even see the tomato seed or know for sure that it's there and

that it will grow. And yet there the seed is, with all the potential that it needs to become a mature plant, gathering power to rise up once the spring comes. These qualities of unknowing, stillness, and a deep underlying power and potential are all associated with Winter. In this powerful silence we are called to listen deeply. Thus the sense associated with Winter is hearing. From the Winter comes the gift of listening without judgment to the great mystery of being.

Now envision the Spring: The days are getting longer and warmer. Overnight, all at once, that tiny little tomato seed has pushed its way up through the dirt toward the light. The unknowing has come to an end—there is a tomato plant there! We can see it! As the Spring continues, the seedling grows in bursts. Each day brings new leaves and new inches in height as the feisty young plant rises up and up. This pushing, rising quality of newly visible possibility is the distinct quality of the Spring. Sight is the sense associated with the Spring. And from the Spring comes the gift of vision and creating new possibilities.

Now consider with us the peak of Summer. The days are the longest and brightest they will be all year. Our tomato plant is now bushy and full and producing flowers. The plant counts on the buzz and activity of visiting bees and animals to pollinate the blossoms as they touch it. And hence, from the Summer comes the quality of that joyful warmth, that lightness of being, that gift of touch. In Summer, as we come to full flower, we know life as the dance of partnership with those around us, the light of being.

Gentle reader, let us contemplate the Late Summer. The cicadas hum peacefully in the trees, the nights grow a bit longer, and we know that the sweet golden days are coming to an end. The branches of our tomato plant round themselves toward the earth under the weight of succulent tomatoes. With so much abundance of ripe fruit, we give the tomatoes away to all those we nourish. Finally we get to savor the taste of the tomatoes we have tended so long. We reap our harvest and are satisfied. We see that it is good, that it couldn't be better made. The gift of the sense of taste is associated with this season. From Late Summer comes the practice of thoughtful savoring and tender nourishment.

And now it is Autumn. The air we breathe grows crisp. Even if we could not see, or hear, or taste, or touch, we would know it is Autumn by that particular pungent smell in the cool air wafting around us. We must acknowledge that Winter will be here soon. The breathtaking beauty of the changing leaves inspires us, takes our breath away. Our tomato plant is getting ready to return to the earth. Although we may salvage a few last tomatoes, it is time to let the plant go. Some of the fruit falls to the earth, where it will rot. From the Autumn comes the practice of bowing in acknowledgment of life exactly as it is. Also from the Autumn comes the ancient awesome gift of smell, borne on the breath itself.

The Five Seasons are different facets of the One. Whatever we say about this One showing itself as Five is a description of ourselves. The cycle of seasons shows in our daily lives and in who we are moment by moment. At any moment, in every situation we can see this dance of Five. For instance, this cycle shows up when having a meal. At first we are in the unknowing about what we will eat: we are in Winter. We listen to our inner voice and our bodies. Then we see some possibility and make some choices about what we will eat (Spring). We plan the food and the tasks to create it. Then we share the preparation in partnership with others (Summer). We enjoy our time together as we create the food. We satisfy our hunger, savoring the sweetness of the gifts of mother earth (Late Summer). We taste our creations and nourish ourselves. And then we let go of the meal and of our time together (Autumn). We do the dishes. We are ready for the next movement of life.

## A Practice of "Five"

Choose some activity that you do frequently. List all of the steps for doing it, as well as the people involved with you. Note where the gift of each season shows up when doing that activity. Discuss the gifts with one person with whom you partner to do that activity.

Pick an activity around which there is a squawk, for example a child cleaning his or her room. Walk through the seasons and pay attention to which seasons show up easily and which seasons have some stuckness. Discuss the gifts with the child and how to make them more apparent in doing this activity so as to provide greater ease.

# Practices and Parables of the "Five"

## Practicing One

Oneness is the recognition of our unity with all human beings and all of life. Reminding ourselves of the constant presence of One, we begin to see how we are alike rather than how we are different from others. Below are two conversations we generated with groups of kids. These are activities you can create in a moment with one child or several.

### The Bread

We brought a loaf of bread to our circle, set it in the center, and spoke of bread together. Bread doesn't grow on trees or come from under rocks. Bread is a form of nourishment invented by human beings in the dance with nature, including water and plants, grains, seeds, nuts, yeast, fire and a container. It is a creation of the whole human family and traditions. Every tribe on earth makes some form of bread.

The kids all know about bread. Here are some of their stories…

Margie: My grandma taught me to make Irish soda bread.

Dave: I love the smell of hot rolls that my mom makes on Saturday morning.

Renee: Pizza. Who thought of pizza? It's really just bread and tomatoes! It's my favorite food.

Bruce: My grandpa makes cornbread, and when he does the whole family sits around the table together eating it.

Lily: I know a song about bread—"Mama's lil' baby loves shortnin' bread."

Sally: Spoonbread. My mommy said her grandma taught her mom, who taught her how to make it. So my mom is

teaching me. It's a special recipe in our family, and you eat it with a spoon.

Nicholas: My dad puts all our old bread together with milk and chocolate and sugar for a yummy dessert. My friends never heard of bread pudding—they don't know what they're missing.

Irene: When my aunt from Greece makes my lunch, she puts something in some pita bread. It's like an envelope— anything fits there, even peanut butter and jelly.

Ariel: During Passover I eat special matzoh bread; and our grandma makes it into balls in soup too.

Chantal: I took my first communion. It's really just a little round flat piece of bread. Sister Joseph Marie told me that God is in it. That God is in us and in the plants and animals and all of nature. And bread is all of that mixed together.

Daniel: Hamburger buns. My friend Joey and I eat hamburgers all the time. I guess we're really eating bread together. I'll have to tell him!

Alex: My uncle is a baker, and he makes bread into braids and all different shapes. It's awesome. He's like an artist with dough.

Hannah: Did you know that bagels are boiled bread? I went with the kids in my class on a field trip and got to see how bagels are made. It was cool…

We took the one large loaf of bread. Each of us tore off a hunk and then touched it, held it, smelled it, really looked at it, and even listened to it. Then we ate it, all of us together at the same time, tasting and savoring the goodness of bread. We told the kids that in Latin the word for bread is "pane" and the word "companion" means "the one I take bread with." *Com pane*— "with bread." The act of eating bread is the act of sharing companionship. And so we are all companions. The reminder that all human tribes eat bread in one form or another is also a reminder that we all are One, in company with each other and with nature.

We asked the question, "What do you think, dear children—are these separate hunks of bread, or is this one bread in all these different places? Does it make a difference what you say? How could it matter?"

Dominique said, "Well, if I say that's yours and this is mine and that they're separate, then I'm not saying how they're from the same loaf. I might not see how I'm connected to you."

All of life is here in this story of the bread: generational transmission, opening the senses to bread and to life, communion, companionship, unity, diversity, and the Oneness among us.

Jason was very excited after we ate the bread. "One piece of bread in different places— wow, that's great!" And then we used another example:

Dianne told him how the Sufi say: "Would it make a difference if instead of saying there are 6 billion different hearts beating in 6 billion different places, we said there is One heart beating in 6 billion places? We say it makes a difference. We are not separate from one another. We are distinct. And we are One."

Sarah spoke up, "At home this morning I was sad because my friend Jessica moved away to Wisconsin last week, and I knew I wouldn't be able to play with her today. Now I can think that she and I have the same heart beating in two bodies and it's like she's not so far away after all. I'm less lonely when I think like that."

"You can also think like that about someone you might have a squawk or a fight with," Dianne said.

She told them the story about her daughter Caeli and her art teacher, Mrs. Carey.

"Caeli said to me one morning, 'I don't want to go to school, Mommy, I have a stomachache. And besides, Mrs. Carey is mean. That's just the way she is.' I could see that Caeli's suffering—her body—was related to her story, her 'squawk,' with her teacher. I asked Caeli to go to school that day and find one thing that wasn't 'mean' about Mrs. Carey. Caeli agreed to do this. When Caeli came home she didn't mention her stomach. When I asked her what she noticed about Mrs. Carey she said, 'I had fun in art class today. And Mom, Mrs. Carey has blue eyes just like I do.' When Caeli made that one observation about Mrs. Carey, that one observation about something they shared, she was able to get to Oneness again with her teacher. From there she had more ease, more freedom just to be with Mrs. Carey."

Much of our unnecessary suffering and illness comes from seeing ourselves as separate rather than as One, interconnected with others. Practice oneness and connectedness, like Caeli and Jason and Sarah, and observe if it makes any difference.

## Sophie and the Circle

Katherine: "Sophie, aged barely a year old, is a teacher of mine, by my say-so. At one point during a SOPHIA for Kids workshop, she came into the room to be with her mama, Melora (our *Alive and Awake* artist). Immediately, every pair of eyes, adult and child alike, was looking at her. Sophie was so vibrant a phenomenon of life in that moment that we were no longer attentive to the activity we were doing together and the conversation we were creating. In that instant, I learned from Sophie something new about the incredible power of life, the phenomenon of *being,* pure and simple. No story, no conclusion. An adult is no less a pure phenomenon of life than a baby, yet somehow I am more practiced at seeing Sophie for who she is. Yet even with Sophie, unless I stay awake as an observer, I could perceive Sophie as just a kid interrupting the program we were doing. Instead, I make Sophie my reminder of the generations. In her presence, even the youngest child in the room that day was her elder. I realized in a new way that these children are the elders of the generations to come."

When considering any action or word, it is a Native American tradition to ask, "Will it honor the parents, the parents' parents and the parents' parents' parents? Will it serve the children, the children's children and the children's children's children?" Each of us sits in the midst of the generation between the ancestors and the children. In choosing to attend to life this way, we see that Oneness includes every creature on earth at the present moment as well as those in the past and future. Always consider that we are One with the seven generations and notice how we can shift our perspectives and actions. You hold the center of these generations, and sit as one with the elders and the youngers.

Katherine: "I gave a speech at my graduation ceremony. I was very nervous at the prospect of speaking in front of hundreds of people. I kept asking myself: 'What's worth speaking? What's worth the gift of their listening?' I realized I had been entrusted with no less than the duty of honoring the ancestors and serving the children. I now have a practice that I designed then to remind myself that my real purpose was to speak for the generations. Beside my word processor, I put a picture of Sophie sitting on my shoulders, pulling my hair and laughing. This was my wake-up call to be aware of the children and the children's children. Next to that I put a picture of my great-great-grandmother, 'Ma Kate,' as a reminder to honor the ancestors with whatever I speak. As soon as I began to look at my speech with the generations in mind, I had much more ease. For Sophie's sake, I can do anything required to serve. And in gratitude to the lineage from which I come, anything I do must be an honoring. With this practice of the photos, I move past my personal concerns. It was so powerful for me that I even crafted it into my speech. I brought both photographs with me to the podium and opened my talk that day by telling those assembled about Ma Kate and Sophie. I said then, and declare now, that the foundation of all my speech, thought, and actions is to honor the ancestors from

*Ma Kate (above) and Katherine with Sophie (below)*

whom we have come and to serve the children and the children's children and the children's children's children."

**Suggested Activities**
Take a loaf of bread and break it into five hunks. Put those pieces in different parts of the room. Then ask, "Do we have five pieces of bread or one loaf of bread in five different places?" Help the child(ren) think into the implications of one and five.

# Practicing Two

Two is the dance of yin-yang. It is the Oneness showing itself as two. Sometimes we experience stuckness and opposition that is actually our deep longing to be reminded we are One with each other. What follows is a teaching story that illustrates how Dianne danced a problem into an opportunity, a squawk into an offering with a kid, Luke, who was in an upset. You will notice that she does not increase the opposition and upset by pushing against him. Rather she speaks to remind him, gently yet powerfully, of his connection to another with whom he is upset.

## Luke and Marge

Dianne: "No way, no way," he shouted. " I hate her guts."

This was Luke, age 11, speaking. I had asked him if he could imagine the possibility of bowing to his teacher. He, along with 20 other kids, had just spent time silently in small circles, bowing to each other one at a time—a practice of the gift of the Autumn. I am thinking it will matter what I choose to say in this moment. Everything that occurs can be used as part of what I craft with him, and all the children are listening. What I say will matter to everyone present. It is crucial in this moment not to fight the upset, the outburst, but to embrace the situation exactly as it is. I must be, I choose to be, One with Luke exactly as he is and practice partnership (Two) with him. Luke had constructed a conversation full of conclusions that he did not recognize as such. He thinks that his story is the way life is.

So here is what Luke and I created together, using his outburst as the starting point:

"Luke, will you talk with me about this?"

"Okay" he said slowly while watching my face.

"What is your teacher's name, her first name?"

"Oh, I don't call her by her first name."

"No, but she does have one, doesn't she? What is it?"

"Marge."

"Luke, do you know what parentheses are?"

"Yes."

"Now, I know you've got some stories about Marge, about how mean she is and how you hate her guts and all that...yet, just for a moment could you put parentheses around all those stories, and we'll scooch them over there." With that I motioned to the other side of the room. "You can always go back later and get them. Just for now, would you put parentheses around those old stories and scooch them out of the way?"

After hesitating a moment or two, Luke said,

"Yes."

"Good. Now, Luke, earlier this morning you said you were alive and awake. Are you still alive and awake? What do you say?"

"Yes."

"Now stay with me on this: Is Marge alive and awake? She could have died in the night, but as far as you know, is she alive and awake?"

"Yeah, I guess so."

"Could you say that the two of you are alive and awake at the same time?"

"Yes."

"Luke, could you bow to her simply because you are alive and awake together?"

After a few silent, thoughtful moments,

"Yes" he said.

All the kids spontaneously burst out clapping and cheering!

Then, I turned toward them all and asked, "Who says it is a possibility to bow to your teacher?"

"Luke says so!"

This declaration is crucial. Who says? We each have a chance to say as long as we have breath with which to speak. Life is not over yet.

"Who else says so?" I asked. "Olivia, what do you say? Timothy, what do you say? Jennifer, what do you say? You each have a say, and what you declare matters."

Everything said is said by someone; it is how we build the world. The Tao according to each child is an offering spoken by each. Luke had, in the presence of all the other children, willingly constructed this new conversation with me in which Marge, simply as a phenomenon of being alive, could begin to show. And here is the choice: Luke in the old reactionary stew, suffering and stuck in the relationship with his teacher Marge; or Luke in a new way of being, a practice of bowing to her exactly as she is, alive and awake. *He* gets to say! Our intention in calling Luke to his teacher's first name is not so he will call her by her first name. It is to remind him that she has a first name, just as he does. They are equal beings of the human sort together. A great practice: find out the first name of whomever you are with in a given moment, such as a waiter at a restaurant. If it is appropriate, call him or her by that name out loud. If it is not appropriate, you can think of him or her by that name silently, to remind yourself of being in practice and partnership with that person *personally*.

Two weeks later, to find out what difference this experience had made for Luke, we asked his mother what she had noticed. She had talked to his teacher Marge, and Marge told her that Luke had come to her and said, "I don't work as hard for anybody else."

We offer this teaching story to you as an example rich with the distinctions of being alive and awake, as embodied by Luke. It contains all the "bones" of this old-new, ancient-modern philosophy. The Oneness of Luke and Marge, at first not easy to discern, is brought to light in Luke's final declaration. The partnership of the Two of them in the dance of being alive together shows as a teacher-student duo. We can see the stuckness and suffering when the rice pot lid (Three) remains clamped down or blows off, rather than easily rising up and coming down as the rice cooks. Suffering and misery arise when we forget the Oneness and go into opposition with someone or something in life. And yet even the squawks are expressions of partnership—if there is someone to observe that. We can forget that Two is only ever an expression of One. Essentially, we forget to bow to life exactly as it is. In this old Chinese wisdom, the starting point, the ongoing embodied practice, is a bow, no matter what, to the oneness of being, even as life shows in all its myriad ways. Who will be awake and alive to declaring the Oneness in the ten thousand manifestations? Will you? Will I?

> *O me! O life! of the questions of these recurring...*
> *...you are here...*
> *and you may contribute a verse.*
> —Walt Whitman

Is anybody a stranger? We asked the kids, "If you are alive and awake and the person you are with is alive and awake, can this person be a stranger? What do you say? No matter who it is, instead of calling this person a stranger, could you call him or her a fellow traveler, alive and awake at the same time? Does what you say matter?" The Dalai Lama has said that the definition of a stranger is a friend whom I have not yet met.

## Activities

Ask the child(ren) to tell you the name of someone with whom they have a squawk (are upset with), either now or in the past. Ask questions about that person: Is he or she alive now? Does he or she eat breakfast, lunch, or dinner? Does he or she sit, stand, or walk? Ask the child(ren) if they (the children) can bow to (acknowledge) that person just for being in the world at the same time as the child(ren). Use similarities to help the child(ren) see the possibilities of "dancing" (working or being together) with that person.

In a group of children, choose one and ask him or her to stand in the middle of the group. Ask the other children how that person is like them. Ask the children on the outside to bow to that child exactly as he or she is. Rotate the children one by one into the middle.

Tell a story in which the main character has a conflict with another. Use a real-life story from your life or the life of someone you know, if possible. Ask the child(ren) how they would "bow" to that person if they were the main character. Encourage them to use their imaginations to create ways to see the similarities and positive aspects of the other person.

# Practicing Three

Three is the creative moment that occurs as life moves—as the rice pot lid bubbles up and down. What follows is a teaching story about a moment of creation with the kids. It was a moment when things appeared not to be moving, when Dianne called the kids into creation with her. Not only that, she called them to observe that they create realities with their words.

**Naming**

Dianne: During an afternoon workshop, I looked at the kids around the circle and saw a phenomenon that I would call "sleepiness." I observed yawns and a few droopy eyelids. And I thought I better do something quick, so we created an imagination game—the naming exercise!

I picked up a sneaker and said, "What else could we call this besides 'sneaker' or 'shoe'?"

Kids who hadn't spoken up before joined the discussion. They called out...

"butterfly!"
"onion ring!"
"cup!"
"eyelash!"
"dead body!"
"two-eyed toad!"

I asked them, "Who says so? Who calls this a two-eyed

toad rather than a sneaker?"

"Ean says so!"

"Jillian says so!"

I was calling them to see phenomenon and then the naming of the phenomenon, to recognize that someone calls it something and someone else listens and says "okay," and before you know it the phenomenon becomes a thing, named.

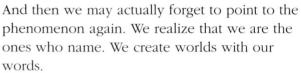

And then we may actually forget to point to the phenomenon again. We realize that we are the ones who name. We create worlds with our words.

Everything I used in this naming exercise was a creation that somebody had made—sneakers and cans of soda and chairs, for example. These things don't grow on trees—all are part of human invention. Names, words don't grow on trees either. All we human beings make sound with our bodies and breath—words are a sure sign of humans, being. We are given breath, we make language.

Each time we do SOPHIA for Kids we take the naming exercise described above one step further. We remind the kids of their own names, their own existence as unique phenomena. Each child goes in the center of the circle one at a time to say: "My name is Jillian and I'm alive and awake!" Then we all shout, "Who says so?" "I Jillian say so. I am here, alive and awake!" This is a proclamation, a declaration from each of us that we are here, named, have a name we call ourselves, that others call us, and that we have a say in being here. The simple declaration "I am here, alive and awake," is a powerful practice any time as a reminder of being here in existence, this day in creation, this moment in time and space. Exactly as we are. "Alive and awake" includes all our ways of being—all the moods and squawks. It is a reminder of the practice of declaring "I am alive and awake" as we are awake to being here, now, in this once-only, will-not-happen-twice moment.

**Suggested Activities:**
Pick an object and ask the child(ren) to say the name associated with it. Then ask them to give it another name. Help them make up "nonsense" syllables to create the name. Ask if the object is different if they give it a new name.

Shakespeare said, "A rose by any other name…" Ask the child(ren) if a rose was called a "yuck," would they like it as much. Explore their responses.

Have one child stand up and say his or her name. Have him or her repeat it until it becomes just sounds. Ask what other sounds could be used to refer to that person.

Choose a word such as "school." Have the child(ren) write down any words or thoughts that they have when they hear that word. Have the child(ren) read those words out loud, one at a time. (If working with only one child, have the adult also write down words associated with "school.") Bring the child(ren)'s attention to the different words associated with school. Ask if the word "learning" has different associations for each of them. Explore how different people hear a word and have different meanings or thoughts. Ask if they can create new ways of speaking about "school" that allow more ease in their bodies.

# Practicing Four

We exemplified Four by asking the kids where they were born and where their parents and grandparents were born, so we could see that the four directions are represented in our ancestors' travels and starting points. Another good way to experience this aspect is to play the game "Six Degrees of Separation." If you want to get a letter to someone on the other side of the earth from you, it could take only five passes from hand to hand, maybe six at most—someone you know to someone who knows that person in another place to another person, and so on. The kids in this one room, through their parents and their parents' parents, represent all the different parts of this one world: Alaska, South America, Africa, India, China, Canada, France, Italy, Ireland, Hawaii, Japan…the North, the South, the East, the West. Someone is always in the place to which you need the letter to go. The four directions *connect the whole earth, and all the places in the world.*

## Our Birthdays

We arranged five vinyl circles, each a different color, in a large circle. Each colored circle corresponded to a season of the year: the red one for summer; yellow for late summer; white for autumn; blue for winter; and green for spring. Each of us called out when we were born and stood on the circle of our birth time.

And oh, the stories of the beginnings:

Melissa: It snowed hard. There was a blizzard the day I was born.

Peter: I didn't have any hair.

James: I peed straight up at my dad.

Emily: My brother and sister were there; I was born at home.

Erin: I weighed five pounds.

Noah: I had the hiccups.

Taylor: My mom hollered and pushed me out.

Scott: I was almost born in my aunt's car.

And the endings: "I wonder on what day I will die?" "Where was I before I was in my mommy's tummy?" I don't know, you don't know, together we don't know the answers to these questions. Death is a mystery. Birth is a mystery. Being alive is a mystery. No one can be born for us, no one can die for us. We must be here ourselves with each other's help. No one can take our place in being alive.

This song is from a children's album, *Teaching Peace*, by Red Grammer:

### "Placcs in the World"

*These are places in the world…*

*Some you know and some you don't*
*Some you'll visit and some you won't*
*Some are near and some are far*
*Some sound exotic like Zanzibar*
*'Cause these are places in the world.*

*Bombay, Cape May, Mandalay, Baffin Bay*
*Baghdad, Leningrad, Ashkabad, Trinidad*
*L.A., Norway, Paraguay, Monterey*
*Singapore, Ecuador, Bangalore, Baltimore*
*These are places in the world*

*Fiji, Sicily, Nagasaki, Tennessee*
*Cairo, Quito, Borneo, Idaho*
*Taiwan, Dijon, Saigon, Teheran*
*Guatemala, Oklahoma, Argentina, North Dakota*
*These are places in the world*

*Some are new, some are old*
*Some are hot and some are cold*
*Some are low and some are high*
*Some are wet and some are dry*
*'Cause these are places in the world*

*Glasgow, Oslo, Fresno, Tsingtao*
*Faukland, Auckland, Yucatan, Disneyland*
*Libya, Namibia, Romania, Pennsylvania*
*Bora Bora, Walla Walla, Costa Rica, Bratislava*
*These are places in the world…*

*Krakow, Changchow, Moscow, Tokelau*
*Dominique, Pikes Peak, Mozambique, Bitter Creek*

*Warsaw, Moose Jaw, Saskatoon, Cameroon*
*Haifa, Mecca, Bethlehem, Jerusalem*
*These are places in the world*

*High on the mountain, down on the plain*
*Deep in the jungle in the middle of the rain*
*Children laugh and children play*
*Everywhere, everyday*
*'Cause these are places in the world!* *

**Suggested Activities**

Ask the child(ren) who they know who lives far away. If they don't know anyone, ask who they know—a school friend or neighbor—who has family that lives far away. Where are they from?

Have the child(ren) ask their parents and grandparents where they were born. Use a globe to find those countries. Look at the distance between where the child(ren) is (are) living and where their ancestors were born.

# Practicing Five: Awakening Our Senses

The five seasons in Chinese thinking have correspondences to each of our five senses. The first way to open to the seasons and all of life is through our ability to listen, see, touch, taste and smell. All that we know about life, we know through our five senses. Sitting right where you are now, what do you hear, see, feel, taste, smell? What do you observe? Sometimes we take our senses for granted. Yet we can actually practice hearing, seeing, touching, tasting and smelling at any time. When we get into a squawk or an upset, we can use practices that we design—practices using our senses—to call ourselves to pay attention to the phenomena of what is so rather than our conclusions about the upset. What are some possibilities or practices with each of our senses? One way to practice is through something we do in SOPHIA with both kids and adults called the Sea Creature (see page 42).

As we awaken our senses we are more open and available to the gifts of each season: the deep power and strength promised by the winter; the clarity and possibility borne by the spring; the warmth and partnership accompanying the summer; the nourishment and thoughtfulness connected with the late summer; and the gratitude and acknowledgment held by autumn's precious beauty.

## Suggested Activities

Close your eyes for each of the first four activities.

Focus on your ears. Everyone be very quiet and listen to what you hear in the space around you. Have a discussion of what each person heard and how different hearing is without using eyes as well.

Focus on your nose. What smells do you notice? Can you simply observe the smells, or do you make up stories: "I like this," or "I don't like that." Discuss the smells each of you noticed.

Next, pay attention to the sensations under your fingers. Touch objects (and people) around you respectfully. Describe what each of you noticed. Is it different to touch without seeing what you are touching?

Have a number of different edible objects. Take turns putting one of them in the other person's mouth. Discuss what each person noticed when a new object was put into the mouth. What showed up when your eyes were closed and you tasted something?

Most people use their eyes a lot every day. Divide the group into partners. One partner leads the other around the room with his/her eyes closed. When the person with his eyes closed is near an object, have him open his eyes for five seconds. Do this three different times. Switch roles. Create a discussion about what showed up when the person opened his eyes and saw an object for a few seconds.

• *These Are Places in the World* from the recording TEACHING PEACE
© 1986 Smilin' Atcha Music. Written by Red and Kathy Grammer.
Distributed through Red Note Records 1-800-824-2980, www.redgrammer.com.

# The Sea Creature

Once upon a time, in a time before time, there existed a great endless ocean and a tiny Sea Creature. This Sea Creature had a permeable membrane skin through which the water of the great ocean flowed in and out. With this skin membrane, it could touch all of life. The Sea Creature also had two openings through which to listen, two for seeing, one for tasting, and two tiny little ones for smelling. These are openings for the Great Sea. We have learned to call them by the word "senses." We have named them "eyes, ears, nose, mouth, flesh." They are how we come to know that we exist. They are how we come to know that we are beings alive and awake. They are how we participate in being alive. The only distinction between the Sea Creature and the great sea of existence is this permeable membrane and these openings.

Now get into pairs; choose someone you don't know. Sit close, across from each other, and choose who will be (A) and who will be (B), and make sure you know each other's names. You are a Sea Creature. Sit with your eyes closed and remember that the great sea of life is flowing through you, all of you, each of you, easily and peacefully. All is well in your little permeable membrane self with these openings for life—these gifts—these senses of listening, seeing, touching, tasting and smelling.

There are infinite numbers of ways to practice with our senses and endless possibilities to design openings. All practices serve to remind us that we are the observers for life and that our senses are gifts. The Sea Creature is a reminder to give our senses as gifts to one another. We asked kids about instances of using their senses. We asked for stories—parables—of moments in which they were particularly aware that they have senses.

# The Sea Creature Listens

From the depths of winter, the great waters, the deep stillness, comes the silence, the sense, the phenomenon we call listening. We know life through listening. Keep your eyes closed.

(A) will be practitioner. (A) keep your eyes closed. (B) open your eyes and lean forward and say to (A) "Hello (your partner's name), my name is (your name)." (A) simply listen—here is the phenomenon; there is no need to react. Simply offer the gift of listening to the unique sound of life of the Sea Creature across from you. Let this sound flow through you like water flowing through the Sea Creature in the great sea of existence. Do this two times, once in each ear, pausing after each round to listen to the silence as well as the sound. Then (A) and (B) can switch roles, and (B) will be practitioner while (A) speaks the same instructions as before.

Jason, age eight, comes for acupuncture treatments. Sometimes he fights with his older brother Sam. Dianne asked Jason to listen to the sound of Sam's voice, separate from the words:

"Just listen. What happens when you just listen to the sound of his voice?"

She was asking him to design a practice using his sense of hearing. Dianne called Jason to give the gift of his listening. Jason's listening is a gift to Sam: he doesn't owe it to him and Sam can't earn it. It is a gift to give our listening to another. The next time Jason and Sam got into a fight, Jason remembered what Dianne had asked him to practice:

"Sam's voice got louder. I thought before that he was being mean, but maybe his voice was just getting louder 'cause he wanted me to hear him better. When I thought of that I didn't get so mad back at him. That time we didn't start hitting each other, and my mom didn't get mad too."

Rebecca, age 10: "I used to get very scared during thunderstorms. I would hide my eyes under the pillow from the lightning, but the sound of the thunder could get so loud that I'd get really scared. A couple of years ago we were visiting my aunt and uncle at the beach, and there was this bad storm. I started to get really afraid. Then my Uncle Pete taught me a special way to listen to the thunder. He said to count the seconds between the flash of lightning and the sound of the thunder, and that way you could tell how far away the storm was. The longer the time between the lighting and the thunder, the farther away the storm was. I sat listening on Uncle Pete's lap, and I got kind of interested in the sound of the storm. I was so busy listening and counting, I *almost* forgot to be afraid!"

Marina, age 14: "At camp we played a game our counselor, Liz, called 'Listening to Silence.' We all lay on the floor so we weren't touching any other kid. We were as still as possible. At first some kids were cracking up and making snoring sounds and stuff. But after a while it got really, really quiet. I heard a lot of sounds I hadn't noticed before, like a plane flying over and birds chirping. It was amazing because then there was this soft sound in the room. The counselor had dropped a pin on the floor! Then she rang this bell—it was cool because I heard the sound for a really long time after she rang it. It seemed like it was hanging in the air. Then it was really quiet again. I did this game when I got home with my friends. They thought it was going to be weird, but they liked it. My friend Mary said, 'Let's make some more silence together.'"

## The Sea Creature Sees

Next, from the great rising Ch'i of the springtime comes the gift of seeing—the phenomenon "to see"—the wonder of sight.

So, Sea Creatures, each with your eyes closed, be fine exactly as you are. (A) practitioner keep your eyes closed. (B) open your eyes. You are going to be looked at—a gentle moment of being seen. Now (A), open your eyes and see your partner. See the life shining through. Look into your partner's eyes for about 30 seconds of clock time. Then both close your eyes and go back into your unique Sea Creature self, your little permeable membrane with the sea flowing through. All the wonder of life is present here in this little moment of seeing. Do this two times, pausing and closing eyes after each moment of seeing. Then switch roles so that (B) is being seen and (A) is the practitioner giving the gift of seeing.

Dianne: "After my dad's death when I was nine years old, my brother Jerry and I went to live in St. Joseph's Orphanage for one year. This allowed my mother to go to beautician's school and learn a skill to make a living to support all of us—her six children. Monsignor Luker became my friend, my counsel, and my practitioner. He didn't use needles—he used his senses. Monsignor saw my downcast eyes and my shoulders hunched forward. He listened to my barely audible voice and heard the assessment of Sister St. Ann who concluded that I was 'painfully shy.' 'You look me in the eye, little girl. You're as good as anybody,' he insisted. And he designed a practice for me to use my eyes. He gave me the task of answering the doorbell and greeting whoever came to visit. It required me to practice looking others in the eye. He called me to be 'eye to eye and toe to toe' with him."

Gena, age 12: "In art class we had to draw a really detailed picture of a leaf. At first I thought it wouldn't take that long to draw the leaf. Then the more I looked at it, the more I saw how complex all the veins were, and the edges around it."

Professor J.R. Worsley, speaking to an acupuncture class:
*The day you really see a tree, you will weep.*

# The Sea Creature Touches

From the great fires of summer comes the gift of touch. That we are enfleshed and have bodies to feel with, that we are literally *incarnate*, is a phenomenon. We are the embodied existence of life. Like the sun, the warmth of life shines through us unique Sea Creatures.

Close your eyes, being fine exactly as you are. Now (A) is practitioner—open your eyes. (B) keep your eyes closed. (A) lean forward and take one of (B)'s hands between yours. (B) let them take your hand; don't give it to them, simply let them take it. Now (A) hold this hand—not a caress, just a simple touch. All of life is here in this wondrous gift. Experience the life living in this hand. Who is this? Then return your partner's hand to their lap. Then (B) be practitioner and take (A)'s hand two times, just as your partner took yours.

Dianne worked with little kids ages two to five at a Montessori Head Start program:

"Some of them were used to touch by hitting each other. You could say they were practiced at hitting. So we practiced a different kind of touch. One child would lie down with the others kneeling around him. Then the other kids would touch him, slowly, quietly, and gently with just one finger. The child lying down would have the experience of being touched in this soft, still way. The children touching him would observe what was different in themselves and their friend when they practiced touch differently. Joey, age four, said, 'I feel like smiling when I touch with one finger as slow as I can.' LaKeisha, age five, told her grandmother later, 'I was scared lying there with the other kids around me. Then when they touched me like that, it was okay and I wasn't afraid any more.'"

Lionel, age 11: "Around Halloween I like to go with my friends to this haunted house. What they do there is you go into a dark room and you can't see anything. Then you touch all these different things. You put your hand in a bowl full of these round squishy things that they say are eyeballs—but they're just grapes with the peels off. It's fun because when I can't see with my eyes, I can sort of see with my hands."

Renee, age eight: "When my baby sister was born, I was kind of nervous to touch her. I could see the spot beating on the top of her head, and she had a scab over her belly button. I was scared I would hurt her. Then my dad showed me how to hold her carefully. Now I even help give her a bath. She is very soft."

Timothy, age 10: "Last summer, my dog had puppies. We got to keep them all for a while 'cause they were too little at first to be away from their mom. One of my favorite things was to lie down on my back and let all the puppies come around me, licking my face and climbing all over me. Even if I was in a bad mood or mad at my mom or whatever, when I would feel the puppies touching me with their little tongues and noses, I would start to feel better inside too."

> *Oh for the touch of a vanished hand...*
> —Tennyson

## The Sea Creature Tastes

All open your eyes. From the great golden late summer, from the sweetness of the earth, comes the gift of taste, of savoring. Each of us is a unique produce of life, like the fruits and vegetables. In this moment we will not actually lick each other (although we could!). However, we will savor each other as gifts from the earth in this way:

First, (A) is practitioner. You will ask (B) the question, "Where in nature do you most love to be?" (A) ask this of your Sea Creature partner and *really* want to know. (B) just respond. (A) savor the gift of nature, the fruit, of the creature before you. Imagine that beautiful place that (B) loves. After one or two minutes of clock time, both of you close your eyes again. Go back into your unique sea-creature self. Observe being, with the great sea of life flowing through you. Then reverse A and B, with B as practitioner, and follow the same instructions.

In SOPHIA for Kids, each child brought a little something to eat to share with one other child. They took turns blindfolding each other and then feeding each other the snack they had brought. The intention was not so much that they guess what the food was, rather our aim was to awaken them in the moment to observe the sense of taste, savoring the gift of food.

Freddie: "I tasted sweet—a cookie."

Sam: "It was salty and crunchy."

Jennifer: "I smelled the orange when she unwrapped it, then she put it in my mouth!"

Fahid: "At first I was worried it would be something I didn't like. Then I thought, 'It's only one bite,' and I just had fun!"

Lynn: "It was cold and sweet—then I realized it was watermelon."

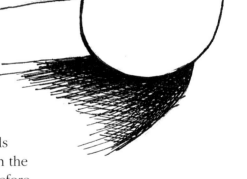

To really feast on the watermelon, ponder how it comes into being: As a seedling in the earth it grows into a glorious plant fed by the sun, rain, earth and the minerals of the soil until its fruit is ripe enough to be plucked. Then the pink succulence of it is savored by the person tasting it. Before our dessert becomes a cookie, sugar from the sugar cane grows out of the earth; wheat ripens from the grains of the fields and is milled into flour; chocolate comes from the cocoa beans; butter is made from the milk of cows; and water comes from the cycle of the heavens and the earth. The cultivation of all of these "ingredients" is a human endeavor. And men and women transport these fruits of the earth to places where cookies are made by other beings of the human sort.

To deeply delight in any food, trace it to its moments of origin, from its beginning through to the moment in your mouth. This is a great conversation to have with our kids: "Where did this food come from?" We can ask this at any moment when food is present, be it an after-school snack or Thanksgiving dinner.

Josh and his mom, Rena, used the Sea Creature to help see food as a phenomenon. Josh's mom was concerned that Josh was "not eating." As it turned out, Josh *was* eating; it was just that the things he was eating were different from what others in his family liked to eat.

Josh said, "I think I was born into the wrong family. I like pepperoni pizza and hot dogs, and everybody else likes vegetables."

"Josh, would you be willing to go to the supermarket with your mom and help her with the shopping?"

"Okay."

"Is that fine with you, Rena?"

"Yes."

"When you go to the market, pretend you are a Sea Creature and practice using one of your senses each time you go. For instance, the first time, use your eyes and pick foods (not packages) that you would like to eat that are different colors—some red food, some yellow, some brown, some white, some blue, some green and so on. Then the next time find foods of different tastes—salty, sweet, sour, spicy, a bit bitter. Play with it and find foods of different textures, smells, even foods that will make different sounds! Then see what you notice when you eat the foods at home!"

Josh and his Mom agreed to practice this way of selecting food. Rena noticed that in fact, Josh *was* eating. And Josh willingly ate some broccoli with his mom, as his "green" thing. There is now more peace at home and in the grocery store!

# The Sea Creature Wafts

From the wonder of the autumn comes the gift of smell. Each of us wafts into life a special fragrance—a unique quality and beauty, as awesome and as worthy as the rose or the violet or the oak tree. Through the phenomenon of smell we inhale life. We breathe each other in. We open ourselves to the awe of the phenomenon of the breath of life itself. Everything has a smell. And by this sense of smell we know life and bow to the wonder of it. This is the practice of simply breathing in the phenomenon of the other.

(A) is the practitioner and (B) closes her eyes. (A) stand up and lean forward toward your Sea Creature partner. Inhale and breathe in your partner's unique presence, the way you would take in a special flower. This is wafting them in. (B) allow yourself to be wafted. Allow yourself to *be* exactly as you are.

Lena, age two, stood near a pile of hand-me-down clothes. She picked up a little shirt from the pile and lifted it to her face, breathed deeply, and said "Cindy! Cindy!" Cindy had, in fact, given her the clothes, and Lena knew this by her nose!

Forte, our puppy, uses his nose as a way of being. His snout is his guide to the trees, to pooping spots, to peeing places, to his fellow dog travelers, to bones, to everything.

"Mary, what do you know by smell?"

"I know where I am by what I smell. I know when I'm on a horse farm, Mommy. I can smell the horses."

After riding, Mary tries to go as long as she can without washing her hands so the smell of the horse will be with her as long as possible.

Katherine: "As a kid at summer camp, I was very homesick. My grandmother sent me a care package. I still remember what was in that package—a flashlight and some batteries, a pin in the shape of a turtle, a pink bandana and a flannel shirt. Wafting up from the shirt was the unmistakable smell of my grandparents' house. I burst into tears of homesickness. And yet I was comforted by the smell at the same time."

## The Sea Creature Comes Full Circle

Now spend some time letting your Sea-Creature partner know what you observed. What did you open to? What phenomenon did you newly observe? What did you notice about how you are with each of the senses—hearing, seeing, touching, tasting, wafting? Are you more practiced with some, less so with others?

Sea Creatures, be sure to thank your partner as we come full circle. Ask first, "Will you allow me to thank you?" The acknowledgment can be as simple as saying "Thank you" and receiving the response "You are welcome."

# THE GIFTS OF THE FIVE SEASONS

Now that we have practiced opening our senses, we can perceive life more clearly and distinctly. From this place of keen observation, we can make gifts to one another. Here we will move through all five seasons, practicing the gifts of each, even as we practiced the gifts of the senses with the Sea Creature.

## AUTUMN

Acknowledgment and bowing to the breathtaking beauty of life, exactly as it is, are gifts of the autumn.

### The Bow

Katherine: Through Bernie I learned something about bowing to another. In SOPHIA for Kids we created small circles of everybody there—kids, teen helpers, and grown-ups. Each of us took a turn in the center of the circle where we bowed to each person there, one after the other. Dianne showed us a gesture that she had learned as a gift from her friend Boye. It is a Native American tradition of gently tapping our chest two times with a lightly-closed fist, and then putting the fully opened hand flat against the chest. This signifies "gift received." As each person received the Bow from the one in the center, each made the "gift received" gesture. Every person, whatever his or her age, received and gave a bow, just for who they are, a fellow traveler alive and awake at the same time in life. Bernie was in my group. As he bowed, he smiled, blushing, and held his body in such a way that I concluded, "Bernie is a bit embarrassed." And yet whatever his personal consideration was, he bowed anyway. It was very still in the room. Afterwards, Bernie said, "If we'd done that in school, there would've been kids laughing and talking during it. It's never really silent in school—the teacher yells 'Quiet! Quiet!'" In Bernie's presence, I was inspired—he had pushed through his embarrassment and his old stories; he was present to me in the moment; and he offered a thoughtful observation. I was moved when I saw the simplicity and dignity of the children as they bowed to each other and to their elders, and their elders bowing to them in turn.

Our intention in bringing the bow to the children is to teach them that there is no one who could not use a bow, and no one who does not *deserve* a bow—just for being. We bow to the essence of who the other is, even if that person has ways of being we don't necessarily "like." There are lots of ways of bowing: a simple thank-you, a salute, a bending of one's head, or taking a breath together are a few examples.

After the day of SOPHIA for Kids, Susan (a mother—three of her girls had participated in SOPHIA) told us that she had been doing dishes when two of her daughters, Olivia and Dominique, had come into the kitchen calling, "Mom! Mom!" to get her attention. When she turned around they asked, "Will you let us bow to you?" She said yes, and her two girls bowed to her, very slowly and reverently. Then Dominique said, "Now do this, Mom, so we know you got the gift," and showed her the Native American "gift received" gesture. Ah! The generations in respect and awe!

*Look at them cows – there's never a bad arrangement.*
—Pa, the Farmer

## Suggested Activities

Design three different ways to acknowledge someone important in your life. Choose a person (your mother, teacher, etc.) and think about how he or she would like to be acknowledged. Some possibilities: give a bow, create a card, make a meal, say "thank you." Think through with the child(ren) when and how each of these acknowledgements would best be received.

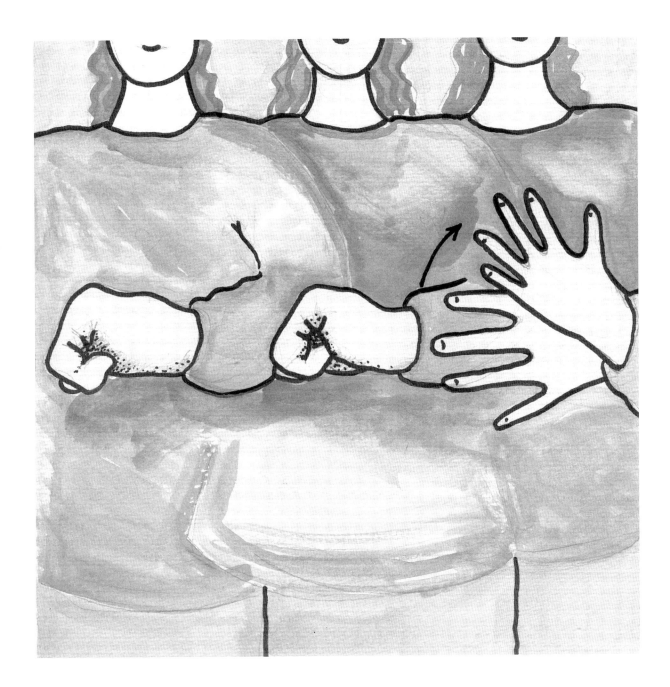

Name someone with whom you have a squawk. Design a way to acknowledge that person, really sincerely acknowledge him or her. Perhaps, find something about the person that you admire—his or her hair, smile, laugh, for example—and design a way to acknowledge the person for that attribute.

# WINTER
### Jillian and the Kernel of Corn

Think about how seeds stay in the dark quiet of the ground before bursting in the spring. Think how a bear will run around eating berries and honey all summer and hibernate in a deep sleep in its den all winter, or how a cat will crouch low to the ground with only the tip of its tail twitching before it pounces. We beings of the human sort are nature, too. We are still and quiet. Stillness and movement go together. Observe this in yourself.

**Popping Corn: An Experience in Stillness and Movement**

Stillness giving birth to movement is a crucial distinction in Chinese philosophy. One way children of all ages can experience this distinction is through a simple moment of popping corn.

    You will need:
a candle (larger than a tea light or votive works best)
vegetable oil
unpopped popcorn kernels
a teaspoon
an eyedropper

1) Place one drop of oil on the spoon with the eyedropper. This itself requires quiet focus. It is important to use the right amount of oil—too little and the popcorn may burn, too much and the oil may splatter.

2) Put the popcorn kernel in the drop of oil on the spoon and hold the spoon over the lit candle.

3) Now hold still with the spoon over the flame. Stay steady with the spoon just the right distance from the candle—too close and the candle will go out, too far and the popcorn won't get hot enough to pop. Wait and watch carefully. Shhhh. Be still.

4) Pop!

5) Eat the popcorn and savor it. (Imagine making a whole bag this way and then eating it!)

There is no movement without stillness, or stillness without movement. In the same way, there is not day without night, top without bottom, front without back, warm without cold, dark without light, up without down, Summer without Winter. Popping the corn is a way to perceive the dance of yin-yang in the world. As human beings we are one with this movement of nature. Vigorous movement naturally arises out of stillness and silence, and once it has reached its fullest expression it gives way to stillness once more…this is the alternating pulse of life.

We each took a turn popping our kernel of corn. One child declined the experience at first, "I'm afraid," he said. "I don't know how." He waited silently for a long time, quietly watching the other kids. Often, a time of quiet and unknowing is needed before doing something new.

Jillian was the last child to pop. We all stood around her while she held her kernel in the spoon over the flame. No one spoke. We waited and waited many breaths of time. It seemed like forever. Was it EVER going to pop? Then all of a sudden— POP! Out of the little kernel came an enormous, fluffy, perfect piece of corn! We whooped and cheered. Her pop belonged to all of us—as in baseball when one person hits a home run, everyone comes home. In life, the bases are always loaded.

# SPRING

## The Stand of Trees

Many of us tribes of humans use a tree as the symbol of life. Trees stand with their roots deep in the earth and their branches reaching up toward heaven. We humans are each the ongoing dance between heaven and earth. Just as each tree is unique, each of us has unique gifts to offer. One tree doesn't look at another and think, "You should be more like me." We don't ask or demand to get a pinecone from an apple tree, or an apple from a lemon tree. Each yields its distinct, unique fruit. So do we.

Practice being a tree. In SOPHIA we often stand in a circle, making a stand of trees, and then look around at each other, standing like trees. We plant our feet firmly on the ground and imagine that we have roots reaching far into the earth. We reach our arms up to the sky like limbs to the sun. In this way, each child experiences her body as the connection between heaven and earth. We close our eyes and shout "Yes!" as we draw our bodies downward and and hold ourselves in a crouched position. Then, we open our eyes wide and spring up tall, reaching up and out with our arms like tree limbs to the sky, and again shout "Yes!" In that moment we learn something

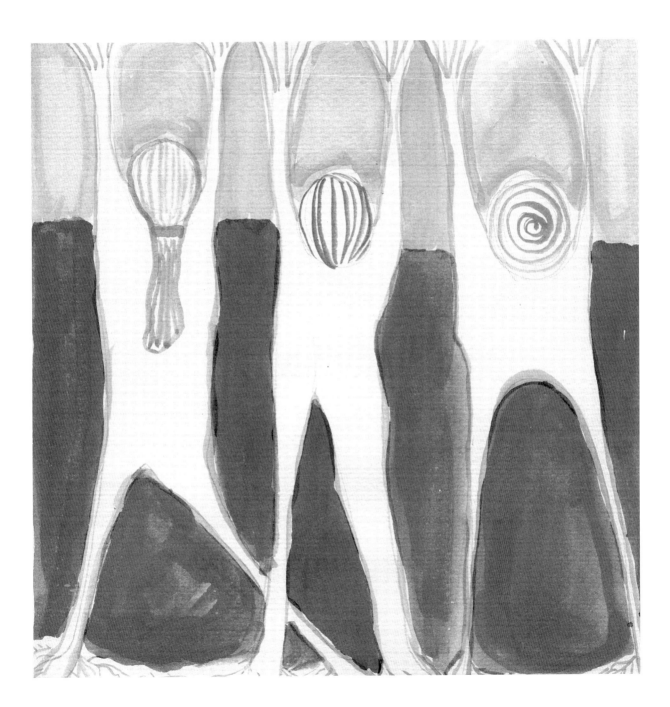

about ourselves as alive and awake, each making our unique sound, uttering the "barbaric yawp" (as Walt Whitman said) of being alive.

Annie: "I have a maple tree. She lives in the front yard of my house. In the early spring, she is my tree to tap for sap to make into maple syrup. She is mine and I am hers. She shows me that, like a maple tree, I'm unique in all the world. Like her, I stand between the heaven and the earth.

"She is my teacher. In the springtime wind and rain she bends and sways. As I watch, I learn to bend in the wind without breaking. Just as my maple is unique, there is not another human being in all the world the same as me.

"In the summer, my maple tree, my teacher, gets big and green. As I stand beneath her, I get cool while the sun shines on top of her and the earth holds her steady.

*Drawing by Bernie Huddlestun*

"When I hug my maple tree in the late summer, she is already turning colors. I remember that transformation is happening all around me and that I am changing, too.

"In autumn I love my friend, my teacher, my tree differently while her beautiful leaves change colors and fall to the earth. I gather her foliage into piles on the earth and play in the crunch. I smell the smells of autumn. I bow.

"It gets colder in the air, and my teacher's leaves are all on the ground. Then I hug her and look up and see limbs of different sizes and shapes against the sky. In late winter and early spring, it will be time for me to tap my maple tree and gather her sweet sap in a bucket. Then spring will come, and she and I will continue our dance, beginning all over again, newly.

"Celebrating the living of my teacher-tree, I reach up toward the sky, toward the heavens, and I bring my branches down to the earth and shout 'Yes!' to all the ways my tree is alive and reminds me to live. Then I bring that grand and exuberant 'Yes!' up from the earth and back to the heavens."

Ask a child:
"What sort of tree might you describe yourself to be?"
"How are you like a tree? How is a tree like you?"
"Could you, would you find a special tree to be a friend? It could be a tree near your home or in a nearby park. Or the tree could be someplace to visit through the seasons; perhaps you could draw pictures of it at different times of the day and different times of the year."

Encourage the child to use all his or her senses with the tree—seeing it, touching it, savoring it or tasting its fruit, smelling it, and listening to the sounds it makes, observing for whom it is a home.

A friend, Joan, was frustrated with her son Joey. She was grumbling to herself about how Joey would "throw a fit" when she was talking to someone on the telephone. She was tired of being upset and fighting. She thought, "This is not effective. What else can I do? What can I practice with Joey?" She remembered the Sea Creature and the part about looking into each other's eyes. So she used that practice the next time she was on the phone and he was squawking. She paused her phone call and said, "Let me look into your eyes, Joey. Give me your eyes." And she held his gaze for a few brief moments. She began to observe that he got quiet, often going off to play, and she could finish her phone call. She was calmer, too! It is such a simple thing to give our eyes to another—the gift of simply seeing each other that comes from the gloriously visible springtime.

*All the universe resounds with the joyful cry—I am.*
—Alexander Scriabin

## Suggested Activities

Ask, "What kind of animal would you like to be?" Listen to the answers and then ask, "How would you act if you were that animal?" Allow the kids to let their imaginations soar.

Ask, "If you were a plant, what kind of plant would you be?" Ask each child to describe what he or she would look like in the springtime. Have the children create an artwork of themselves as a plant.

# SUMMER

## The Blanket

Dianne: "In SOPHIA for Kids, most of the children have not met each other before. We play a game where we all sit in different places, scattered about the room. The kids close their eyes at a given moment, and one of the adults takes a blanket and covers up someone in the room. The game is then to look and see who shows up as missing from the group. I was amazed at how observant the kids were at this game. Although they had not known each other before that day, they knew who wasn't showing almost immediately. The notion of "showing up as missing" is important. No one *is* missing, they *show up as* missing. Things and ways of being can show up as missing. We are not equally practiced in all ways of being. We are already whole, nothing is missing, and there are always new practices to take on.

I think about Amnesty International. One of the actions reported to be most powerful for a political prisoner is to receive a letter written specifically to them when imprisoned unjustly and in life-threatening circumstances. Sometimes the letter or note that can be gotten through to the person will simply say, "We know you're here. We know who you are. You are not alone. You are not forgotten." Former prisoners often report that it "saved my life" to receive those notes, helping them to have the courage and strength to stay alive in prison, to not go crazy or get sick. That simple note, a statement of partnership, has a huge impact.

These kids offered partnership and camaraderie to each other in the "blanket" game and through other simple actions such as a smile or a wave—actions that signaled "We know you're here." They reminded me of Amnesty International: human beings taking care of each other through simple statements and letters that indicate "We're aware of you. We know who you are. We haven't forgotten you."

## Alice and the Standing Ovation

An ovation is a whoop, cheering, acclamation, fanfare, jubilation, tumultuous pleasure, an enthusiastic outbreak of applause, a celebration of a triumph. In SOPHIA for Kids, we use it as a celebration of the triumph and gift of being alive.

Alice, age 13, stood on a chair while the rest of us stood around applauding her with clapping and cheering and hooting. We delivered to her the gift of a standing ovation, celebrating that she is here. Just that—that she exists exactly as she is. She stood very still with her hands clasped in front of her and her head down. And then, Alice smiled. Like the dawn breaking!

> *Joy is the infallible sign of the presence of God.*
> —Teilhard de Chardin

## Suggested Activities

Draw a picture of yourself and someone with whom you have a partnership (this could be a family member, friend, teacher). What are you doing together in your drawing? What else do you do together?

Design a way to let someone know you're glad they're alive. Some possible ways: give them balloons, bring them flowers, draw a picture for them, etc. Allow for individual creativity in this activity. Have the child(ren) present the product of their joy in another's beingness to that person. Later discuss whether their offering created joy and how it showed up.

# LATE SUMMER

## Kiss the Booboo

Dianne: What is the greatest healing act?  When asked, "How do you do what you do?" Mother Theresa of Calcutta said, "I know how to wrap a bandage, and I love. I know how to clean a sewer, and I love. How to write a bank draft, and I love." She used an oozing sore as an opportunity to love. Kiss the one who has the booboo, not just the booboo. Kiss the booboo all the way through. My Mama Irene, 84 cycles of seasons, called everything that hurts a holy bump. From stubbing my toe to an upset with my friend, everything needs to be kissed, even when it hurts and maybe even especially when it hurts. Every hurt is a holy bump if you can see it that way—if you say so. There are many ways of kissing a booboo.

Booboo, owie, squawking place, hurt—all the kids had some version of the same idea. We used the word "booboo" as little children do, to mean all the hurts, the stories of pain—body and soul. We spoke of booboos, scars, old hurts, broken bones, a kind of "who has had what" session:

Bill: "Once I fell from a tree and couldn't breathe. I thought I was dead. My dad picked me up and held me."

Debbie: "I had an earache that hurt so bad. My mom rocked me all night long."

Marc: "I was running and felt a sting on my foot. I stepped on a bee. I was crying and my Uncle Steve carried me in to my mommy's lap and got the stinger out."

Alec: "I had a loose tooth and my daddy wiggled it for me. It was just dangling. I was afraid he would yank it, but he didn't. Instead he gave me a drink of water and told me to swish it around in my mouth. Out came that tooth! It didn't even hurt or bleed. My daddy is so smart."

Claire: "My brother had a cut that was bleeding, and my grandma took a cobweb and put it on my brother's arm. She said the spider knew how to make a bandage before people did."

Joey: "I had to get my tonsils out and I was scared. My sister Annie told me that when I wake up after my tonsils are out, some kind ladies in white would be there to give me anything I wanted—especially ice cream—and so not to be afraid. And when I woke up, there they were, just like Annie said! Ice cream never tasted so good!"

Ivan: "I got hit with a flying baseball bat and broke my nose. My grandpa rigged up an ice-pack. What a shiner I had—it turned so many colors."

Peggy: "My finger got caught in my bicycle chain. It was really bleeding and it hurt. I cried and my brother let me wipe my tears on his sleeve until my mom came."

Steve: "One night I had a fever of 105. I was so hot I was seeing things. My dad said it was hallucinations. He and my mom put me in a tub of ice water to cool me down. They were scared 'cause I'd never been so sick before. I liked my dad holding me afterwards, and I love to tell the story. He remembers it too."

A little practice: Consider the way a sore heals. See the way a cut bleeds, forms a scab, dries up and falls off until just a little mark remains. A little scar is a reminder of a moment of life that hurt and healed.

### The Gift

*To pull the metal splinter from my palm*
*my father recited a story in a low voice.*
*I watched his lovely face and not the blade.*
*Before the story ended, he'd removed*
*the iron sliver I thought I'd die from.*

*I can't remember the tale,*
*but hear his voice still, a well*
*of dark water, a prayer.*
*And I recall his hands,*
*two measures of tenderness*
*he laid against my face,*
*the flames of discipline*
*he raised above my head.*

*Had you entered that afternoon*
*you would have thought you saw a man*
*planting something in a boy's palm,*
*a silver tear, a tiny flame.*
*Had you followed that boy*
*you would have arrived here,*
*where I bend over my wife's right hand.*

*Look how I shave her thumbnail down*
*so carefully she feels no pain.*
*Watch as I lift the splinter out.*
*I was seven when my father*
*took my hand like this,*
*and I did not hold that shard*
*between my fingers and think,*
*Metal that will bury me,*
*christen it Little Assassin,*
*Ore Going Deep for My Heart.*
*And I did not lift up my wound and cry,*
*Death visited here!*
*I did what a child does*
*when he's given something to keep.*
*I kissed my father.*
                    —Li-Young Lee[1]

A few years ago at the Seattle Special Olympics, nine
contestants, all physically or mentally disabled, assembled at

the starting line for the 100-yard dash. At the gun, they all started out, not exactly in a dash, but with a relish to run the race to the finish.

All, that is, except one boy who stumbled on the asphalt, tumbled over a couple of times, and began to cry. The other eight contestants heard the crying. They slowed down and looked back. They all turned around and went back to the boy. Every one of them. One girl with Down's Syndrome bent down and kissed him and said, "This will make it better." Then all nine linked arms and walked together to the finish line.[2]

*Notes:*

1. Li-Young Lee, "The Gift" from *Rose*. Copyright © 1986 by Li-Young Lee. Reprinted with the permission of BOA Editions, Ltd.

2. This teaching story from the Special Olympics has appeared anonymously in a variety of contexts.

# SONGS

*If you can talk you can sing.*
*If you can walk you can dance.*
—A saying from Zimbabwe

Every tribe of beings of the human sort has sound. Every tribe has rhythm sounds, reminders of heartbeat, of lifetime happening. Every song is sound carried on breath like wind. It is not possible to sing without breath to carry the sound. Song is breath time, our lifetime happening. And oh, how many songs there are: with words, without words, songs to work by, songs to pick berries, to sow seeds, to sew garments, to gather the harvest, to sing to our babies, to sing to our gods and to each other, songs to live by, songs in a round, in solo, in concert, songs from all countries, in all languages, holy songs, sacred songs, rowdy songs, profound, profane drinking songs, patriotic songs, songs for the open road, songs of animals, of birds, of whales, of insects, songs of the day and songs of the night, songs of morning and of evening, birthday songs, songs for the dying, songs for bearing what we must, croonings, cooings, chantings, songs taught by elders to youngers as we come and go.

*Row row row your boat, gently down the stream,*
*Merrily, merrily, merrily, merrily, life is but a dream.*

This is one of those songs that mamas sing to their babies, generation to generation. We sing it together in a round, a song of life with no beginning and without end, a circle of song reminding us of being, all always one.

Dianne: "We sang 'Row Row Row Your Boat' at my dear friend Dede's funeral. I remember the sound of her laughter—she laughed a lot. When she got sick, we would sing this song together. Dede liked to hear the 'life is but a dream' part. I miss her."

*Brother Al-Duba sings a favorite song.*

## Sharing Memories about Song

Jade: "My grandma sings 'Barnacle Bill the Sailor' to me, and I sing it with her to my little sister. Grandma pretends she is Barnacle Bill, and I pretend to be the fair young maiden. It is one of the things I love most…to sing with grandma."

Maureen: "'And I'd give the world if I could hear her sing that song again…' is from an Irish lullaby. When I hear it or sing it, I cry. My mom died when I was seven. I don't remember much, but I do remember her singing 'Tooralooraloora' from that Irish lullaby."

J.J., who comes to Dianne for acupuncture treatment, uses a song of joy ("Zip-ah-dee-Do-Da") as a practice when he gets into a reaction or a mood in school. He designed singing the song for himself as a reminder not to fight. What is a favorite song that you could sing in any given moment to remind you of another way to be?

Dianne: "I sing 'Danny Boy.' It's a song that remembers love and mortality. I use it to keep perspective on what I'm up to at any given moment. And I sing it to my babies, as a gift."

Katherine: "My song is 'You Are My Sunshine.' I cry at how precious we are to each other, at how much I love being alive with you."

And you, dear reader? What do you say? What is your song?

*Will there be singing in the dark times?*
*Yes there will be singing about the dark times.*
                                                    —Bertoldt Brecht

*Life is not a one-walk dog. You can't take that dog for one long, long, long walk and think, "There, now I've done it." You've got to walk that dog every day!*

# KIDS AS PRACTITIONERS

## The Charlie and Maggie Practice

Maggie's sister Carrie died the day before our last SOPHIA for Kids. Maggie is Charlie's mom. She chose to honor her sister by spending the day with Charlie and bear her sorrow with all of us present. Maggie spoke of her sister in the circle of the children at the beginning of our day together. Charlie piped right in, "And her friend, Tammy Walker, died two weeks ago. She's also crying about that." Dianne asked Charlie what he did to assist his mama in her suffering. "Well, I hugged her." "What did you notice when you hugged your mom?" "She stopped crying for a little while." Maggie showed all of us one way of being with the awesomeness of death. Cultivating together the art of living, of bearing what we must, and of dying, we dance together. Charlie's tenderness for his mama in her sorrow is a gift, a practice.

## Caeli and her French Laugh Practice

Katherine: Dianne, Caeli and I travelled together to Heidelberg and Rome. One night at dinner, we were listening to a family speaking French at a nearby table and Caeli popped out an imitation of Gallic *joie de vivre* that we came to affectionately call "Caeli's French Laugh"—a throaty yet somewhat nasal emanation made with a mischievous grin. The more Caeli did her "French laugh," the more we laughed with her.

Later on in the trip, my wallet showed up missing in the Milano train station. I was pretty upset and involved with my stories of "Where could it be?" "What happened?" "If only I hadn't..." Caeli said, "Katherine, should I do my 'French laugh' now? Would you feel better?" "Yes, Caeli, *please* do your 'French laugh' now!" And so she did, helping to make what could have been a tortured, moody, and worried eight-hour train ride across the Alps much easier for all of us. This was a wonderful moment of Caeli, age nine, being practitioner to her friend Katherine, age 30.

From then on during our journey when any of us would be on an edge—on the edge of hunger, the edge of tiredness, the edge of our wits—losing our observer one way or another, Caeli would do her "French laugh" and we'd all lighten up again. We'd come back from our reactionary stew, any grumpy story line to some bit of brightness, some lightness of being. And if Caeli herself was in a bit of a squawk, one of us would ask her to do her laugh and she'd start to come out of it. She keeps her "French laugh" as a practice even now at home.

## Luke Accepts the Call to Partnership

Dianne: Toward the end of the day Luke was lying on the floor, separate from the group. He was not smiling.

I said to Luke,

"Will you come back to the circle?" and he said,

"No, I'll just stay here."

So then I took a single piece of paper (to demonstrate Oneness again) saying,

"This is One sheet of paper. Now I'm going to tear it into these five different pieces. We could call them five different pieces of paper in five different places. We could call it One piece of paper in five different places. I, Dianne, say with all of you that it matters to call it One piece of paper in five different places. I say, let's say it's One."

I then took each piece to a different place in the room, putting one down next to Luke.

"Is Luke One with us exactly where he is?" I asked the kids. They all said,

"Yes!" Then I said to Luke,

"You are fine exactly as you are, and we are together in the circle. Thank you for your partnership, Luke."

"You're welcome."

## Offerings from the Children

We asked, "What's a gift, one thing, from our time together today that you could give to another person in life with us? It could be a word or a picture on paper with magic markers; it could be anything you say."

Tyrell: "My grandma sings songs with me. I'm going to tell her how we sang here today. She'll like that."

Vicki: "I drew this picture of the tree in my backyard for my dad. He planted it when I was born. It's my tree."

Faizel: "Here's a picture of me bowing to my mom. She's gonna be surprised!"

Jason: "The next time my baby sister Becky cries, I'm going to listen to the sounds she makes instead of yelling. I'll pretend she's a Sea Creature and just listen for a minute."

# REMINDERS TO PRACTICE

## Stones

We asked each child to bring a stone, a special rock to give away to someone else. Stones are formed from the press of the earth. Rocks, gems, jewels, beautiful stones—all are made from the earth and are older than we are. We all have "rock stories"…

> Jack: "My mommy wears a diamond ring."
>
> Irene: "My sister got a ruby for her sixteenth birthday."
>
> Ginger: "Sometimes my dad puts on gold cuff links."
>
> Carol: "My teacher has jade earrings."
>
> Carl: "I saw the Hope Diamond at the Smithsonian Museum."
>
> Dianne: "Elise brought me a black and white stone from Tibet shaped like a yin-yang."
>
> Katherine: "The stones in the North Sea are rubbed so smooth and round."

You are as beautiful and valuable as a jewel, though not as old. A rock can be a reminder:

Dianne said, "Keeping a rock in my pocket (especially if it's at least a one-pound rock!) is a way to remember to stay awake to being alive."

Luke's mother told us that Luke keeps his rock by his bed.

## Twigs

The kids went outdoors on a search for a twig—a twig to bring back as a gift from nature. One at a time we put our twigs into a basket in the center of the circle: "I, Ashleigh, bring this twig as a reminder to give gifts to life." We are gifts from life, to life. Then we passed the basket around the circle, each of us taking a twig as a reminder.

## The Doll

There is a Native American tradition known as the talking stick. The one who holds the stick is the speaker for creation, which alerts all the others to be the listeners for creation. In the Native American tradition, this person speaks to bring the day into being. In SOPHIA we designed a version of the talking stick by using a little doll with no face—and therefore *all* faces. All those not holding the doll are alerted that we are there listening for the speaking, the listeners for the speaker. "I built a temple deep in their listening." (Rilke) Without the listening there is no place to speak into. We do not owe, nor can we earn, the listening of another—it is a gift. So is the speaking. At some moment during the day, each child took the doll to make an offering with his or her speaking. By the end of the day, everyone had spoken.

## The Practice of Poetry

Read poems with kids—memorize a poem together. Here's one to start: "The Pasture" by Robert Frost.

### The Pasture

*I'm going out to clean the pasture spring;*
*I'll only stop to rake the leaves away*
*(And wait to watch the water clear, I may):*
*I sha'n't be gone long. — You come too.*

*I'm going out to fetch the little calf*
*That's standing by the mother. It's so young,*
*It totters when she licks it with her tongue.*
*I sha'n't be gone long. — You come too.*

# For Further Reading…

*All Sickness is Home Sickness*, Dianne Connelly

*The Law of the Five Elements*, Dianne Connelly

*To Come to Life More Fully*, John Sullivan

*Dumbing Us Down: The Hidden Curriculum of Compulsory Schooling*, John Gatto

*The Giving Tree*, Shel Silverstein

*Freddy the Leaf*, Leo Buscaglia

*Seven Arrows*, Hyemeyohsts Storm

*Harold and the Purple Crayon*, Crockett Johnson

*Growing Without Schooling*, John Holt

*The Sense of Wonder*, Rachel Carson

*Old Turtle*, Douglas Wood

*Winnie the Pooh*, A.A. Milne

*Ivan Illich in Conversation*, David Cayley

*Woolgathering*, Patti Smith

*Teaching Peace*, Red Grammer

*Leaves of Grass*, Walt Whitman

*Oh, the Places You'll Go!* Dr. Seuss

*Tao: The Watercourse Way*, Alan Watts

*The Illuminated Rumi*, Coleman Barks (Translator)

*Rose*, Li-Young Lee

*How to Read a Poem and Fall in Love with Poetry*, Edward Hirsch

*Love You Forever*, Sheila McGraw (Illustrator), Robert N. Munsch

# Acknowledgments

**Dianne and Katherine Together:**

For Sadie, our great mama, who raised up lots of babies, not just the ones born through her body. She taught us all that we are one, whatever our size, shape, color, age, or place of birth. We would also like to thank Alexis, Alice, Allyson, Amy, Ashleigh, Asia, Barbara, Bernie, Billy, Blaize, Bob, Boye, Brian, Brooke, Caeli, Carol, Charlie, Christella, Christy, Dawn, David, Dede, Diana, Dominique, Ean, Edie, Elise, Erica, Gail, Gillian, Graeme, Gus, Haig, Hans-Peter, Harwood, Jack, Jade, James, Janet, Jennifer, Jim, Joan, John, Josh, Judy, Jumel, June, Kelly, Kevin, Lennox, Lisa, Luke, Maggie, Malaya, Mallory, Martha, Mary, Mary Ellen, Matt, Megan, Morris, Nancy, Olivia, Pa, Pauline, Preethie, Rae, Ralph, Sabrina, Sally, Sam, Scott, Sean, Shirley, Sophie, Stella, Susan, Suzanne, Tamar, Terri, and Ysaye.

Melora, through your eye and hand, little squiggles and great swirls become reminders of joy in being alive, all of us as kin. How generously you "Yes!" us. Artist, we bow to you.

John, "By their fruits you will know them." This book, this fruit of our work together, has been designed into being by your caring skill. All our ancestors will be honored. Our children will be served. On their behalf, we thank you.

Julia, you *are* the Sea Creature, the wonderful sweet powerful presence of Oneness between Heaven and Earth. The only distinction between each of us and this great sea of life is this little permeable membrane skin and these openings we call senses. Thank *you. Thank* you.

Elizabeth, poetry is so close to the unsayable, and yet this is what we say of you—this line from the great wise Solomon's Song of Songs: "How beautiful thou art to me, my love. How beautiful thou art." Elizabeth, thank you for your grace and gracious offerings.

And to Mary Ellen, the very presence of creation itself, thank you. *Word up. World be born.*

**Dianne**:

For Mama Irene—You were courageous for me, for all six of us, your kids—Jack, Peg, Steve, Jerry, Andy, and me. You knew it takes a village, and in our village you called for practices of peace and compassion. You taught me, taught all us kids, to be at peace by what we do and what we say, for the sake of the whole village.

Our beloved Mama Irene breathed out and not in again on March 12, 2000. My breath, through her, belongs to you, beloved reader. I give you this book—from the breath-time that lives me—on behalf of all kids in this world village.

For Katherine, Katarina, Friend, Philia—you in whose presence I come to know myself as more beautiful. Katherine, in your presence I know Life as Good and Beautiful—as Gift. *Grazie, cara amica, anam cara*, for this book and all the gifts you bring to make this dance of existence more beautiful. *Hosanna.*

For Blaize, Jade, Caeli—the fruit of my womb. You are ongoing gifts to me, my wisdom teachers.

**Katherine:**

Dearheart Dianne—I am profoundly grateful for your presence here on earth, for your friendship fierce and true. Thank you for calling me again and again to the deep power and beauty of words.

To my mother, Elise—"child-beguiler" that you are. Thank you for teaching me what love is.

To my beloved Philip—You are a great blessing in my life.

*Dianne and Katherine*

*Dianne M. Connelly,* a practitioner of traditional acupuncture for 32 years, holds a doctorate in the philosophy of medicine. She is cofounder and chancellor of the Tai Sophia Institute for the Healing Arts in Laurel, Maryland, where she teaches and practices acupuncture. Author of *Traditional Acupuncture: the Law of the Five Elements* and *All Sickness is Home Sickness,* she teaches widely in Europe and New Zealand, as well as the United States. She is a graduate of Le Moyne College (B.A.), New York University (M.A.), Union Graduate School (Ph.D.), and the College of Traditional Chinese Medicine in the United Kingdom (Master of Acupuncture), where she studied with Professor J. R. Worsley. Born in South Colton, New York, she lives in Columbia, Maryland, and is the mother of Blaize, Jade, and Caeli, and the grandmother of Tamar and Lennox.

*Katherine Hancock Porter,* a graduate of Swarthmore College, earned her Master of Acupuncture degree from the Tai Sophia Institute where she serves on the faculty. A frequent contributor to *Meridians* magazine and former dean of students at Tai Sophia Institute, Katherine practices acupuncture in Baltimore.

*Melora Scanlon* received a BFA from the Maryland Institute College of Art, and a Master of Acupuncture degree from Tai Sophia Institute in Laurel, Maryland. Melora practices acupuncture in Baltimore; serves on the faculty of the Tai Sophia Institute; and maintains an art studio in Columbia, Maryland. Her paintings are in numerous private collections. Currently she is preparing a book of images that are meditations on acupuncture points. Melora is the devoted mother of Sophia and Stella Rose.